£1·50 (20)

WILLIAMSPORT

SCRANTON

WILKES BARRE

LAKE WALLENPAUPACK

DELAWARE
WATER GAP
NAT'L REC. AREA

SUSQUEHANNA   RIVER

ALLENTOWN

HARRISBURG

PHILADELPHIA

DELAWARE RIVER

STATE & NATIONAL FORESTS - Refer to Pennsylvania Recreation Gu[...]

D1419654

USA, Pittsburgh, PA, octobre 2005

Pour mon plus
grand bonheur Theodor
Gabriel, mon fils qui me rend la
plus heureuse maman du monde
                                    maman

Pentru un mare amator de
plimbări în natură.

            Papa.

PENNSYLVANIA'S Natural BEAUTY

Pennsylvania's Natural Beauty

Text© 1993 by Ruth Hoover Seitz

Photography© 1993 by Blair Seitz

ISBN 1-879441-79-9

Library of Congress Catalog Card Number
92-062897

Published by

RB
BOOKS

Seitz and Seitz, Inc.
1006 N. Second St.
Harrisburg, PA 17102-3121

Designed by Master Designs, Palmyra, PA

Printed in Hong Kong

PENNSYLVANIA'S
Natural
BEAUTY

Ruth Hoover Seitz
Photography by Blair Seitz

RB
BOOKS
HARRISBURG, PA

ACKNOWLEDGMENTS

Enjoyment fosters appreciation and hopefully leads to understanding and protection. For me, this sequence of attitudes emerged as I spent time in the wild. Such childhood endeavors as picking huckleberries and blackberries in the coal hills of Schuylkill County and trying to dam a spring-fed stream in a cove festooned with laurel blooms created a strong visceral bond with the outdoors. Time in Pennsylvania's wild places has forged a primer grasp of the state's flora and fauna, but for this book I relied on the input of knowledgeable naturalists.

I am most grateful to Dr. Larry Klotz, professor of botany, Shippensburg University for his patient sharing of his vast knowledge of flora in the eastern part of the state. The inspiration of Tony Wilkinson, Heritage Program director, and the assistance of botanist John Kunsman, both in the eastern office of the Pennsylvania Natural Diversity Inventory, contributed to this book. From the western part of the state, Paul g. Wiegman, director of natural science and stewardship for Western Pennsylvania Conservancy, gave valuable input.

I also thank many state employees—Sarah E. Hopkins, Nick Kerlin and Ed Deaton of the Bureau of State Parks as well as Edward T. Dix of the Bureau of Forestry and Jerry Hassinger of the Pennsylvania Game Commission. Thanks to Greg Edinger, naturalist at Bowman's Hill Wildflower Preserve, for his guided walks and to Frank Felbaum, Wild Resource Conservation Fund, for his vision for a conservation-minded public. The help of these and many others stirred Blair and me to prepare a book that will motivate others to enjoy and protect Pennsylvania's natural beauty across four million acres of public lands.

—Ruth Hoover Seitz

TABLE OF CONTENTS

Introduction

■

From the rose tinting of the hills by the bloom of red maples (*Acer rubrum*) to the opening of the bowl-shaped flower clusters of Pennsylvania's state flower, mountain laurel (*Kalmia latifolia*), spring delivers delicate designs of growth in Penn's Woods.

■

The sun unleashes energy to feed bright, heady wildflowers that woo butterflies and other insects. Photosynthesis crowns the forests with green plumage. In contrast, in an acidic habitat such as a bog in the Poconos, carnivorous plants ingeniously thrive.

■

After the roadside brilliance of asters (*Aster* spp.) and goldenrod (*Solidago* spp.), the deciduous forests take their turn, showing a foliage palette from flaming gold to plum red. Bird migrations, buck rub and seed dispersal mark the woods folding its energy into a seasonal repose.

■

From a brown bareness that exhibits each weather scar to a snowy blanket that transforms each woodland sculpture, winter safeguards life for spring's bursting. Pennsylvania's earliest flower, skunk cabbage (*Symplocarpus foetidus*), is likely to poke through a late snowfall.

INTRODUCTION

"The clearest way into the universe is through a forest wilderness." John Muir

Since childhood when I walked barefoot upcreek turning over rocks in search of crayfish, I have lived with a special love for the woods and stream. Raised along Stony Run near Yellow Breeches Creek in the woods of northern York county, my home environment included the sounds of flowing water, breezes in the trees and bird songs breaking the country stillness. Traffic and city sirens were distant.

So my forays this past year into the wilderness across Pennsylvania to photograph this book were a homecoming for my native spirit. Camping next to pines along mountain streams awakened my nature instinct. Deeper than the rigors of long 14-hour days and the tiring road travel required to make the pictures was the satisfaction of spending many hours at a waterfall or along streams framed with moss-covered rock. Aware of the miracles of nature around me that had formed over thousands of years, I was pleased to know that the experience of my childhood was still alive, a respite from my urban and more hassled business life.

The wilderness, as John Muir suggests, is a path to our great universe. While sky and sea lie beyond, the woods with many layers of growth, its geological history and myriad species is for Pennsylvanians the most accessible route to the world of natural wonders.

The millions of acres set aside as state or national forests and parks are our treasures to enjoy. I salute those who had the foresight to designate and preserve those large green areas of the countryside. Open the Pennsylvania recreational map, observe the green areas and head out for one of them. Take those gravel roads and mossy trails and explore. You are likely to be surprised and held by the beauty, as I was.

In a year round effort, I have traveled to all of our state forests and 65 of the 113 state parks. I would like to return to Tuscarora, Allegheny and many other wilderness areas to hike more deeply into the forests. Veteran backpackers have seen more than I have. The natural sites that I photographed are accessible to the casual traveler.

In the winter, I carefully climbed the snow and ice-covered trail along the waterfalls of Ricketts Glen, looking closely, observing the ice sculptures and water flow underneath. Snow lay over the ice and tree branches. At World's End and Little Buffalo State Parks snow drifted down over rock formations making a wintry contrast to the blue-greens of the lichens and mosses, and at Laurel Hill State Park, a fresh foot-deep gentle snow heaped mounds on the rocks of Laurel Hill Creek and held the hemlock branches low.

In the spring, I caught the first wildflowers pushing through the brown leaves at Gifford Pinchot State Park. Then I traveled to Shenk's Ferry, Pinehill, Raccoon Creek and Bowman's Hill Wildflower Preserve to find trilliums, trout lilies and dutchman's breeches. I then followed mountain laurel and rhododendron buds into the summer. In areas such as the midstate's Tuscarora Forest, laurel turned the woods into a great garden wedding with more white dancing flowers than royalty would have. At higher elevations the forest floor was covered with the flowering heath as far as I could see.

In July, I found the rhododendron of Rothrock Forest hugging 300-year old white pines and, in other areas, Ohiopyle and Linn Run, for example, these shrubs of white blooms with intricate pink interior etchings were tall and full enough to form snow-like archways over the hiking trails. During the summer, I enjoyed many moments of Pennsylvania's natural beauty from Pymatuning State Park, a waterfowl paradise in the far west, across the state to Dingmans Falls, a waterfall in the Delaware Water Gap National Recreation Area in the far east.

As fall began, I made my fifth trip to the Laurel Highlands where the red maples were now stunning in their true color, and the forest greens had become lighter in a wider palette. In the Northwest, at Presque Isle and as far as Promised Land State Park, I experienced and photographed the excitement of the extraordinary fall color of the state's shrubs, bushes and deciduous trees. One day in dazzling sunlight and the next in a quiet drizzle, I enjoyed the tall, aged timbers of Allegheny National Forest at Tionesta and Heart's Content, natural areas of 300-500 year-old white pine and hemlock.

I took an excursion along the West Branch of the Susquehanna River on Route 120 between Lock Haven and Emporium, one of the state's most scenic fall foliage routes. Hyner View, a panoramic view of the river and mountain ranges, and Kettle Creek and Sinnemahoning State Parks in Sproul and Elk State Forests are along the route. I returned through Quehanna Wild Area of Cameron County, a surprise preserve of tiny, multiple waterfalls and abundant wildlife.

As though a concert had reached its climatic moment, I ended my journeys at High Knob Overlook in Wyoming State Forest. Orange hues glowed in the sky as the sun fell behind the seemingly endless ridges now mostly leafless. I was awed by the beauty as I had been again and again while traversing Pennsylvania throughout the year.

The natural areas that I explored and photographed for **Pennsylvania's Natural Beauty** attract me as strongly as the outdoor memories of my childhood. In the coming years, given several days to get away, I'll take my map and head out for one of those green spots, certain to find a kinship in the wilderness with my native spirit.

—Blair Seitz

ABOVE Otter Creek winds through woods, York County. FOLLOWING PAGES Muddy Creek in York County mirrors fall foliage in its tranquil flow towards the Susquehanna River.

S P R I N G

Weeks before green growth appears in Pennsylvania's wilds, I watch for hints of stirring life and usually find red maple (*Acer rubrum*) buds the herald of spring. A reddish tint slowly coats the gray rolling hills that slant across the state's ridges and valleys. Originating from expanding flowers, this warm tone colors the mountains—a magical promise that a new season is on its way. It is a special season, the one that recharges the growth cycle. With 58 percent of the state covered in forest, this sight is within easy drive of any of the 67 counties of Penn's Woods. On a clear day I cannot glimpse enough of this promise. I feel a singular joy that another equinox has come.

In the state's northwest, layers of burgeoning leafage color winter's dark bareness in the state's largest public wooded area, the half-million acre Allegheny National Forest. After the initial rose hue, an array of greens stretch over the hills from the oaks along the slopes of the

Allegheny and Clarion Rivers up to the ridgetop where cherry and ashes bud last. I like to note the numerous growth changes that take a Pennsylvania forest to full foliage. It is like watching a newborn become a toddler. Despite my intentness, I so easily miss aspects of the unfolding.

Within the woods, bumps characterize the threshhold of spring. Enlarged tree buds signal the wonder of spring discarding the secure brown scales of winter. In deciduous forests, airy with light, maples, beeches, oaks and hickories are festooned with swelling buds and catkins ranging from yellow green to deep wine-red. Down at ground level, tightly coiled fiddleheads poke out of the leaf litter.

In March each male deer sports soft, velvety knobs that become long, pointed, bone-hard antlers by late summer. Among Pennsylvania's elk in Elk and Cameron Counties, one of two herds roaming east of the Mississippi, bulls also grow new racks each year, each antler reaching close to four feet within several months.

Some tree branches birth flowers before leaves. Very early, shadbush or Juneberry, a small tree with white-petaled flowers in the genus *Amelanchier* brightens the understory. The flowers of the spicebush (*Lindera benzoin*) look like yellow lights, and its twigs and leaves bring an aromatic citrus scent to the woods. A little later, with fragile but sturdy grace, redbud (*Cercis canadensis*) blooms burst out of the tree's twigs and cluster on the branches like pink-lavender Christmas lights. I hike in Gifford Pinchot and Caledonia State Parks to see this small tree's bud-draped limbs. They create a pastel etching against wintry background of the woods.

About the same time, flowering dogwood (*Cornus florida*) adds a filigree to the forest. So many of these trees, elegantly donned with large, white bracts, are victims of a fungus called dogwood anthracnose that has been moving rapidly through northeastern United States since 1978.

Before leaves close the overhead curtain, an array of wildflowers sprout on the woodland floor. For a few short weeks, they wave their colorful shapes in the sun's caress. Some of the earliest arrivals are harbinger-of-spring (*Erigenia bulbosa*), hepatica (*Hepatica* spp.) and spring beauty (*Claytonia* spp.) with rose-striped petals that are the height of delicacy.

As daylight lengthens, other wildflower gems bloom. The mottled leaves of the trout-lily (*Erythronium americanum*) hold a pretty yellow bloom. Trilliums (*Trillium* spp.) and dutchman's breeches (*Dicentra cucullaria*) are conspicuous. The blossoms of the May-apple (*Podophyllum peltatum*), wild ginger (*Asarum canadense*) and Indian cucumber-root (*Medeola virginiana*) seem to cower under umbrella-like leaves.

I treasure violets. Their lavender, purple, white and yellow heads dance and nod above their deep green leaves, some of which can add flavor to a spring salad. They are rich in Vitamins A and C. In Pennsyvlvania common blue (*Viola sororia*) and yellow stemmed (*Viola pubescens*) are among this easily hybridized wildflower that has 300 species world-wide.

The rush of spring in Pennsylvania first appears in wetlands, one of the state's most threatened habitats. In marshes and bogs, plants wrest out of the thaw with vigor. Even though half of the Commonwealth's plant species thrive in wetlands, people think of them as mosquito-infested swamps that are full of snakes. As contractors and industries drain or fill in "marshy wastelands" for development, the state loses 14,000 acres of this nurturing habitat each year.

It is understandable that as the state's wetlands decrease, so does the life that depends on them. About 57 per cent of the more than 600 plants on the State's Rare and Endangered Species list are usually found in wetlands. For example, botanists with the Pennsylvania Natural Diversity Inventory track spring-blooming showy lady's slipper (*Cypripedium reginae*) which is classified as threatened because it occurs at only six to 20 sites. Globe-flower (*Trollius laxus*) is considered endangered because this woodland species exists in only one to five locations.

Even plants classified as rare because they may occur at two or three dozen places within the state seldom appear in large numbers. Occasionally, naturalists discover an awesome surprise. While hiking in the mountains of southcentral Pennsylvania, Dr. Larry Klotz, a Shippensburg University botany professor, recalls happening upon a natural pond supporting a spectacular wildflower display. "There were dozens of golden club (*Orontium aquaticum*) in full bloom, with the rich afternoon sun making the inflorescences seem like glowing white candles in a lake of black water." These slender orange-yellow spikes are separated from their green stalks by a white band, a brilliant sight that is most uncommon in Pennsylvania's wetlands.

With the globe losing plants at the rate of two species per day, what other moments of beauty have been missed? Plants provide greenery, oxygen, food and chemicals. They are the source of about 40 percent of our drugs. For instance, digitalis from the leaves of the foxglove (*Digitalis purpurea*) has been a major drug for heart ailments, and three anti-cancer formulations come from the bloom of the mayapple (*Podophyllum peltatum*). But only about five percent of our plants have been analyzed for healing components. What potential cure has eluded science because its plant source has lost a place to live? Pennsylvania's natural habitats are a resource for human sustenance and serenity.

When leaves slowly push out of tree buds and dainty blooms pop out of the forest floor, I am renewed by the promise of spring's growth. I slosh into the marshy spots where the stretching daylight puts on the first act of spring's drama. I can't spend enough time in the woods when warmth elicits a carpet of blue-eyed Mary (*Collinsia verna*) at Enlow Fork in Washington County; a mass of trillium at Wolf Creek Narrows Natural Area near Slippery Rock and a sea of Virginia bluebells (*Mertensia virginica*) at Shenk's Ferry Glen in Lancaster County... treasured ephemeral shows of natural beauty in Pennsylvania.

As spring readies to exit, the bloom of the state flower, mountain laurel (*Kalmia latifolia*), graces Pennsylvania's forests. This heath is widespread, but gives particularly great shows in the Laurel Highlands in the southwest, within the 2,000 square-mile Poconos in Monroe and Pike Counties and throughout the Seven Mountains area in the state's center. The stands that both feed and shelter deer become a mass of frothy, pastel beauty. While hiking, I examine the details of these clusters of pale bowl-shaped blossoms with red coating the bottom. Each flower seems sculpted for both the artistic observer and the pollinating bee.

UPPER LEFT Bloodroot (*Sanguinaria canadensis*), a wild-flower whose red root provided eastern Indians with a bright juice for decorating, blooms in the woods at Gifford Pinchot, a York County state park named to honor America's first forester and trailblazer of the conservation movement. LOWER LEFT At Pinehill, a stream-fed knoll in Dauphin County, a henbit (*Lamium amplexicaule*) erupts from the springtime earth. ABOVE Catkins, a name given to compound blooms because they resemble cats' tails, bedazzle this tree at Centre County's Poe Valley State Park.

LEFT One of the spectacular blossoms of the tuliptree (*Liriodendron tulipfera*) is on a decaying tree stump at Colonel Denning State Park, Cumberland County. ABOVE Newly unfurled leaves and dangling buds of the sugar maple (*Acer saccharum*) signal spring's burgeoning in the forest canopy of Poe Valley State Park, which is surrounded by 198,000-acre Bald Eagle State Forest, Centre County.

PREVIOUS PAGES A newly-leafed deciduous forest paints a spring sky, State Game Lands, Clark Valley, Dauphin Cty. CLOCKWISE FROM UPPER LEFT Receiving sunlight through a leafless canopy, wildflowers pop out of the forest floor. Dutchman's breeches (*Dicentra cucullaria*) flourish in moist, rocky woodland. • Spring beauty (*Claytonia virginica*) is an early bloomer. • Wetland jewels, marsh marigolds or cowslips (*Caltha palustris*) are actually related to the buttercup. • Trillium (*Trillium flexipes*) and Virginia bluebells (*Mertensia virginica*) are compatible Appalachian neighbors, blooming here at Shenk's Ferry Wildflower Preserve, Lancaster County. • Woodland or blue phlox (*Phlox divaricata*) feature wedge-shaped petals, Raccoon Creek State Park, Beaver Cty.

• • • • • • • • • • • • • • • •   19

CLOCKWISE FROM UPPER LEFT A green frog (*Rana clamitans*) feeds on one of the smallest flowering plants, duckweed (*Lemna perpusilla*) in pond at Bowman's Hill Wildflower Preserve, Bucks County. Redbud (*Cercis canadensis*) blooms burst from a twig.

• Halictid bee, a valuable pollinator, alights on wild geranium (*Geranium maculatum*), Game Lands, Stony Creek, Dauphin County. • Red trillium (*Trillium erectum*) bloom stands regally above its leaves on a hillside at McConnell's Mill State Park, Lawrence County. • The blossoms of the shrub pinxterbloom (*Rhododendron periclymenoides*) adorn the woods in May, Dauphin County.

• • • • • • • • • • • • • •

ABOVE With moss (*Dicramum* spp.) gaining a foothold, two species of lichens thrive on diabase rocks, Gifford Pinchot State Park, York County. RIGHT Mountain laurel (*Kalmia latifolia*), the state flower, flourishes in poor, rocky soil across Pennsylvania. Backgrounded by a stand of big-toothed aspens (*Populus grandidentata*), here the heath grows in Tuscarora State Forest, Perry County.

• • • • • • • • • • • • • •

ABOVE Streams of light brighten new leaves and early blossoms, Cowans Gap, Fulton County. UPPER RIGHT A very characteristic bloodroot (*Sanguinarius canadensis*) blooms with pollen on the petals, G. Pinchot State Park, York County. LOWER RIGHT The dogwood (*Cornus florida*) brings ornamental beauty to the forest. Its spring blooms are not flowers in the true botanical sense, but modified leaves. Its hardwood was probably used to make primitive skewer-type weapons; this links its common name to the old English word *dag* which means "to pierce." Cowans Gap State Park is in a valley of the Tuscarora Mountains.

PREVIOUS PAGES A typical Pennsylvania spring view
shows off the crisp new greens taking over the reddish
maple (*Acer* spp.) buds of a deciduous forest. ABOVE In
Forbes State Forest within Laurel Summit State Park,
Somerset County, mountain laurel (*Kalmia latifolia*)
thrives alongside pale-green hay-scented fern
(*Dennstaedtia punctilobula*). Both plants are common and
widespread in Pennsylvania. RIGHT The acid rock soils
that feed laurel (*K. latifolia*) are derived from sandstone
and quartzite. This rock in Tuscarora State Forest is also
an ideal growing environment for this moss (*Leucobryum*
spp.).

LEFT The geological upheaval that cut a gorge into McConnells Mills State Park moved soil and upturned boulders, creating this rock formation in Lawrence County. Ferns (*Polypodium* spp.) and a turf of moss (*Polytrichum* spp.) cover the flat upper rock, and mosses (*Hypnum* spp.) and (*Hygrohypnum* spp.) grow on angular surfaces. ABOVE Mosses such as (*Hygrohypnum* spp.) thrive in cascading streams, here at Rock Run in Linn Run State Park, Westmoreland County.

S U M M E R

It is the sun itself that unlocks this glorious season of many moods. After the music of spring rains, summer features June flowers on stream banks and then the robust full-summer blooms in fields and roadsides.

I wouldn't want to wager whether humans or butterflies most enjoy the presence of such summer wildflowers as evening primrose (*Oenothera biennis*), butterfly weed (*Asclepias tuberosa*), cardinal flower (*Lobelia cardinalis*) and Joe Pye weed (*Eupatorium fistulosum*).

Since evening primrose blooms unfold at dusk, their rich nectar first entices nocturnal moths. When the insects leave, its petals wilt. The open blooms that I have seen in full light are unpollinated leftovers awaiting a daytime visit from butterflies. Each summer night the petals of a few more blooms unfurl for winged visitors as well as human nature lovers. This species looks luscious.

The auspicious orange butterfly-weed flags swallowtails from dry, open spots. I love watching this sun-loving flower in the milkweed family charm butterflies.

Just as brilliant but with a shaggy look, the red cardinal flower is the preference of the hummingbird, which hovers above a blossom, sipping nectar and pollinating this exquisite native wildflower.

I first became acquainted with the regal Joe Pye weed while gathering wildflowers for an August wedding. Bees were very busy on its clusters of pinkish purple flowers. Its common name harks back to an Indian medicine man who gained fame from using it to treat typhoid and several other diseases.

Shade-lovers also flourish as daytime extends well beyond 14 hours. June light first opens the mountain laurel (*Kalmia latifolia*) and then the larger pale-pink rhododendron (*R. maximum*) blooms. Mature stands of this beautiful native heath abound in rain-rich glens in the Delaware Water Gap and along the Allegheny Ridge. They grow comfortably in the shade of hemlocks (*Tsuga canadensis*), a tree whose litter contributes to the acid soil that both need. In Lancaster County's Tucquan Glen, home of one of the state's scenic creeks, I enjoy walking a trail under a canopy of this shrub. Rhododendron is also a companion to red maple (*Acer rubrum*) in another moist habitat, the bog.

In the summer, life fairly percolates in a bog, a Pennsylvania habitat that developed where depressions remained as glacial ice receded about 15,000 years ago. Over the years, these craters filled with rain water and plant forms took root along the edges of these specially-formed lakes. In this placid water, peat moss (*Sphagnum spp.*) floats and forms mats that support other plants. Beyond them grow grassy sedges, low shrubs and then a forest of such trees as red maple, black spruce (*Picea mariana*) and larch, also known as tamarack (*Larix laracina*). From the air, a bog looks like a watery eyeball in the middle of concentric rings of vegetation.

Greg Edinger, an educator at Bowman's Hill Wildflower Preserve, Washington Crossing Historic Park, recalls his first summer foray into a glacial bog in the Poconos. "There's a primeval eeriness to the unique habitat, the reason that the "bog-ey" man supposedly lurks here. In the forest,

I passed hummocks of peat moss over stumps and decaying logs. I then stooped through thickets of rhododendron and dense blueberry shrubs, fighting mosquitoes and bypassing poison sumac.

"But soon I emerged into a more open area and saw wonderful wetland species growing on floating bog mats. Red and yellow dragonflies darted around fragrant waterlilies (*Nymphaea odorata*), spatterdock (*Nuphar luteum*) and orchids such as rose pogonia (*Pogonia ophioglossoides*) and swamp pink (*Arethusa bulbosa*), an endangered flower in Pennsylvania."

Edinger explains why this environment is called a "quaking bog." "It is like walking on a waterbed, but it is natural with thousands of years' worth of spongy vegetation underneath. Spagnum can hold up to 25 times its weight in water; today it is prized by gardeners just as it was used as diapers by Native Americans.

"All at once I plunged through the mat and I was waist-deep in water, yes, bogged down. As I emptied my boots, I noticed several insect-eating plants having lunch. With a vacuum mechanism on their small sacs, bladderworts (*Utricularia* spp.) were sucking in aquatic insects. Nearby, a mosquito was being absorbed into a pouch-shaped leaf of the pitcher plant (*Sarracenia purpurea*). Earlier, the plant's nectar glands had wooed the insect into its deadly solution of enzymes and rain water. Also, a sundew (*Drosera* spp.) had caught a light-blue damselfly on its sticky red hairs. All these insectivorous plants absorb the amino acids of their prey to get the nitrogen that they need. It was really special to observe these adaptations of nature in this untampered, beautiful bog."

Very few pristine bogs remain. To see their magic without getting bogged down, visitors take boardwalk strolls in Centre County's Black Moshannon State Park and through Tannersville Cranberry Bog, a 719-acre section of the Stuart M. Stein Memorial Preserve in Monroe County. The latter is managed by The Nature Conservancy, an international conservation group that has been responsible for protecting plants, animals and natural communities on more than 36,000 acres in Pennsylvania.

Since its founding in 1932, The Western Pennsylvania Conservancy has preserved several wooded habitats among the 173,000 acres of choice natural lands that it has protected west of the Susquehanna River. Among these, Tryon-Weber Woods is one of the finest mature stands of beech-maple in the western part of the state. Many leaves on spreading arms of both of these species create an abundantly shady environment. A mature tree will transpire seven tons of water on a hot day. Since this produces the same cooling effect as ten room air conditioners, it is a boon to be in the forest when the thermometer soars. In its most basic role, photosynthesis in leaves fuels life. An acre of forest produces enough oxygen to keep 18 people alive for a year. For me, the lush green of the season renders untold satisfaction each time I camp or hike under its canopy.

Dry environments also burst out in color in the heart of summer's fertility. On shale cliffs along the Delaware River in Pike County, Pennsylvania's only cactus, the prickly pear (*Opuntia humifusa*), blooms on the poor soil of the face. For centuries, this cactus has cherished the intense heat that builds during each summer on bare shale steeped at a 70' angle. Also, within Jennings Environmental Education Center in Butler County, a small relict prairie remains from a much larger but similar ecosystem that emerged about 2000 B.C. This habitat resembles a Midwest prairie and features the blazing star (*Liatris spicata*), a rose-purple flower that peaks each August.

In open places and deeply shaded forests I feel the heady strength of sun and moisture feeding plant cells that create beauty. I never tire of the common but elegant jewelweed (*Impatiens* spp.) and use its leaves to prevent poison ivy rash. In darkened woods I look for waxy white Indian pipes (*Monotropa uniflora*), artistic mushrooms and new designs of shelf fungi. Each species adds to Pennsylvania's biodiversity, and my time with all the colors, textures and shapes increases my capacity for wonder.

ABOVE Morning sun streams through World's End
State Park, Sullivan County. RIGHT Fallen corollas of
the rhododendron decorate the floor of Rothrock State
Forest, Huntingdon County. Lichens cover tree trunk,
and moss (*Dicranella* spp.) and mushroom (*Amanita*
spp.) sprout near Stone Creek.

PREVIOUS PAGES This summer scene in Alan Seeger
Natural Area in Huntingdon County typifies virgin
forest within the state's forest plateau. This 150-acre
Area has magnificent old hemlocks (*Tsuga canadensis*)
and white pines (*Pinus strobus*), some 300-500 years old.
Among the carpet of mosses is a species (*Mnium hornum*)
that favors stream banks. LEFT Covered with mosses and
liverworts dark, shaded trunks in moist settings take on a
tropical appearance, Rothrock State Forest, Huntingdon
County. Rhododendron (*R. maximum*) blooms in foreground. ABOVE This bloom from a rhododendron
flower details its ten stamens and the patterns and spots
that guide insects to the nectar.

PREVIOUS PAGE Canada geese (*Branta canadensis*) swim in morning fog in Pymatuning Lake, Crawford County; this body of water is within the borders of Pennsylvania's largest state park. LEFT The sun lowers over Pymatuning Lake, which has a 75-mile shoreline. ABOVE A red wing (*Agelaius phoeniceus*) perches on a dead branch in the wetland swamp at Haristown, Crawford County. • An evening glow spans sky and lake after sunset at Pymatuning State Park.

CLOCKWISE FROM LEFT Male Mallards (*Anas platyrhynchos*) survey meal possibilities at Pymatuning Lake. • Cedar wax wing (*Bombycilla cedrorum*) perches on a dead branch at Presque Isle State Park, a peninsula jutting into Lake Erie. • Great blue heron (*Ardea herodias*) focuses on finding aquatic creatures for lunch, Pymatuning Lake, Crawford County. • Goldenrod (*Solidago* spp.) brightens the shores of Middle Creek Wildlife Management Area, which comprises 1700 acres in Lancaster and Lebanon Counties.

PREVIOUS PAGES Endowed with numerous rapids, the Youghiogheny River rushes for more than 14 miles through Fayette County's Ohiopyle State Park, the Commonwealth's second largest state park. ABOVE Bushkill Run plummets through a moss-cloaked area of the Pocono Mountains in Monroe County. UPPER RIGHT A blooming raspberry bush (*Rubus* spp.) grows alongside broadbeech ferns (*Thelypterius hexagonoptera*), Buck Hill Falls, Monroe County. LOWER RIGHT Cucumber Run spills about 30 feet into a wooded ravine, Ohiopyle State Park, Fayette County.

LEFT Hemlocks (*Tsuga canadensis*) and 125-foot
Dingmans Falls beautify Delaware Water Gap National
Recreation Area, Pike County. ABOVE This is one of
the 22 waterfalls that can be seen along a five-mile Falls
Trail at Ricketts Glen State Park, Luzerne County.
Liverworts (*Plagiochila* spp.) growing in the spray zone
like being saturated.

ABOVE The Loyalsock Creek flows through a narrow S-shaped valley in the 780-acre World's End State Park in Sullivan County. RIGHT In Pike County, Little Bushkill and Bushkill Creeks have eight falls. The widest, Bushkill Falls is privately owned and open to the public.

PREVIOUS PAGES The first visible plants to grow on bare rock are lichens. These may be a hundred or more years old, all the while slowly breaking rock into soil, here at Trough Creek State Park, Huntingdon County. LEFT A patch of young lichens (*Cladonia* spp.) grow on a dead tree stump at Hickory Run State Park, Carbon County. ABOVE The alien purple loosestrife (*Lythrum salicaria*) flourishes, clogging the state's wetlands, here at Delaware Canal State Park, Bucks County.

ABOVE Designated nationally as a "Registered Natural Landmark" Bear Meadows Natural Area is a swampy 325 acres with many plant specimens of the glacial bog, Rothrock State Forest, Centre County. RIGHT (*Ganoderma tsugae*), the brown mushroom that looks shellacked, characteristically decomposes dead hemlocks (*Tsuga canadensis*). This moss (*Thuidium* spp.) likes a humid environment, here at Trough Creek State Park, Huntingdon County.

UPPER LEFT Up to two feet in diameter, the leaf of American lotus (*Nelumbo lutea*) resembles a pizza pan perched on a stick. One of two Pennsylvania stands of this North American native thrives at Wildwood Lake, a marsh in Harrisburg, Dauphin County. LOWER LEFT Algae nourish wildlife at Pymatuning Swamp, Crawford County. ABOVE A dragonfly epitomizes speed and agility, soaring, hovering and darting, consuming tremendous numbers of insects. This male blue dasher (*Pachydiplax longipennis*) stakes out his territory between mad dashes to snatch tiny flies out of the air. Bowman's Hill Wildflower Preserve, Bucks County.

ABOVE Fifty nine percent of Pennsylvania's 28.7 million acres is forested. A view of World's End State Park from Canyon Vista confirms the S curves of the Loyalsock Creek, Sullivan County. RIGHT Silverthread Falls is an 90-foot cascade in the Delaware Water Gap National Recreation Area in Pike County.

PREVIOUS PAGES Looking north, Lake Alfred forms a tranquil body before the waters of the Susquehanna River flow south to the Chesapeake Bay. LEFT A white oak (*Quercus alba*) of 300 years spreads its limbs on the border of Marsh Creek State Park, Chester County. ABOVE This field of boulders in Hickory Run State Park, Carbon County is designated as a National Natural Landmark because it is a relic of geological action 20,000 years ago. Some rocks are 26 feet long.

ABOVE An upper segment of Dingmans Falls fills a pool in the Pocono Mountains, Pike County. RIGHT From the shale cliffs called Nockamixon Rocks or High Rocks in Ralph Stover State Park, the view down is of Tohickon Forest and Creek, northern Bucks County.

PREVIOUS PAGES Pine Creek meanders through scenic Lycoming County near Slate Run on its way to the West Branch of the Susquehanna River. UPPER LEFT Layers of algae and lichen-coated rock were broken and stacked by nature's forces, Trough Creek State Park, Huntingdon County. LOWER LEFT Mosses (*Hypnum* spp.) cover fallen log in pine woods, Cook Forest State Park, Jefferson County. ABOVE Stream water feeds the liverworts decorating rocks in the Tuscarora State Forest, Perry County.

ABOVE At sunset rock islands dot the Susquehanna River just north of Harrisburg. RIGHT Of elegant shape, Turk's cap lilies (*Lilium superbum*) are a native species of lily, a plant that has been under cultivation for more than 3,000 years. Here it grows at Bowman's Hill Wildflower Museum, which exhibits the state's flora. UPPER RIGHT Evening sun tints the main artery of the Susquehanna River.

PREVIOUS PAGES Hawk Run (on the right) joins
Mud Run near Hickory Run State Park, Carbon County.
LEFT This view of the West Branch of the Susquehanna
River and Sproul State Forest looks south from the
overlook of Hyner View State Park, Clinton County.
RIGHT Sunset deepens the tones of the ridges of the
Tuscarora Mountains, Cumberland County.

A U T U M N

In the fall Pennsylvania's woods put on an unmatched panorama of color. Forests of mixed hardwoods sprinkled with evergreens can be so beautiful that any romantic from the Midwest would be awe-struck. Even natives proudly praise their state's flaming fall foliage. In September, as the browns at ground level multiply, they heatedly discuss the exact "peak of the trees this year." Any of the first three weeks in October is a usual choice depending on how far north one lives. The timing of color changes also varies from bottomlands to peaks. Using the biological yardstick that 100 miles in latitude equals1,000 feet in elevation, it is safe to say that as people travel north, seasonal and environmental changes occur as if they are climbing higher into the mountains.

"The turning of the leaves" occurs because their chlorophyll breaks up and drains away to reveal the tree's true colors. It happens when photosynthesis, the manufacturing of food and oxygen, stops. Early in the season, the black gum (*Nyssa sylvatica*) and sumac (*Rhus* spp.)and later, red maples (*Acer rubrum)* and scarlet oaks (*Quercus coccinea*) wear reds ranging from ruby to maroon. On the beeches (*Fagus grandifolia*), birches (*Betula* spp.) and ash (*Fraxinus* spp.) species, yellows appear, but the gold of the aspens (*Populus* spp.) are supremely vivid. Each year when leaves close down their food factories, trees perform the most spectacular event in nature in the temperate zone.

Nothing pleases me more than walking into the heart of a wood that autumn draped in a range of golds. In sunlight, the intensity of the color swirls around me, carrying me into its brilliance. And on dense, gray days, the saffron yellow garners light into the heart of the woods, multiplying the glow so that even at dusk, I feel enveloped in brightness.

In short order, wind and longer, cold nights do the work that gives this season its name. Each fall, a year's worth of leaves flutter to the ground. An acre of forest donates two tons of leaves to decompose into soil. But first, each leaf stalk draws a barrier at its end to close off the summer pipelines that carried water from the roots via the trunk and branches and food from the leaf itself.

In damp areas, cinnamon ferns (*Osmunda cinnamomea*) turn pure nut-brown, and in the forest, maidenhair (*Adiantum pedatum*) and, at its edge, bracken (*Pteridium aquilinum*) species change to a tawny yellow. The Christmas fern (*Polystichum acrostichoides*) stubbornly stays green year round. When a rain showers a woods in its fall glory, trunks darken. I enjoy watching these tall, chocolate sentinels rise between the yellows overhead and underfoot.

Before leaves fall, the signs of autumn dominate all wild habitats. Birds migrate in flocks and singles. Erie's Presque Isle State Park, a peninsula that is largely wetlands, is a September stopover for thousands of migrating birds. They forage in the marshy coves and along the sandy beach, an only among Pennsylvania habitats. The browning buttonbush (*Cephalanthus accidentalis*), rose blueberry (*Vaccinium* spp.) leaves and leathery bayberry (*Myrica* spp.) shrubs tidy for winter under the yellow, insect-bitten foliage of sassafras

(*Sassafras albidum*) and cottonwood (*Populus* spp.) trees.

Near Hawk Mountain Sanctuary, a lookout on a knob of Kittatinny Ridge, broad-winged hawks, eagles and other raptors ride the wind, soaring south by their inner calendar beginning in September.

In sunny spots, wildflowers flaunt deep, rich hues as a final fling before frost. Goldenrods (*Solidago* spp.) put out a sun-drenched feast for insects. I enjoy identifying jaunty asters (*Aster* spp.) as they bob their pale lavender and deep purple clusters in the breeze. My favorite is the princely New England aster (*Aster novae-angliae*). It is fun to find the white-petaled calico (*Aster lateriflorus*) after their yellow centers have matured into a dark violet. In marshy soil grow the splendid gentians (*Gentiana* spp.), all a cerulean blue.

David E. Young, a regional environmental education specialist, relishes canoeing through a marsh, one of his favorite Pennsylvania habitats. He recalls the setting. "All was quiet except for the deep, loud screech of the barred owl. I stopped paddling to watch brown cattail (*Typha* sp.) spikes and a beaver lodge outlined in the moonlight. One sundew (*Drosera rotundifolia*) spread its carnivorous leaves, shaped like tiny coins, on a partially submerged log.

"I must have made a sound because, without warning, the beavers that were silently gliding along my canoe slapped their tails, splashing me before they dived to the bottom. I dipped my oars into the water again to head toward the maples along the shore."

Autumn wonder also prevails along streambeds because moss, stones and the water path itself add variety of color and texture to the canopy. Besides, each scene opens a page or two of Pennsylvania's natural history. Tens of thousands of years ago, the southernmost tip of the last glacier, the Wisconsin Ice Sheet, extended to the present site of McConnell's Mill State Park in Lawrence County. Its melting altered the direction of area waterways, and years later, the draining of Lake Arthur carved Slippery Rock Gorge 400 feet deep into rolling countryside. Today its rushing creek, massive sandstone boulders and forest plants stand as a powerful phenomenon of geologic scarring.

The wilderness characteristics of another state park thrill Paul g. Wiegman, director of natural science and stewardship for Western Pennsylvania Conservancy, the state's largest private land conservation organization. "I like to be totally alone in Ohiopyle's landscape. I am intrigued by the variety of vegetation on the faces of the 1,700-feet deep gorge, and below, the plunge of the raging Youghiogheny itself." Wiegman treasures the River's cascading feeder streams in addition to well-known Ohiopyle Falls. Ferns and wildflowers flourish in the park's glens and plateaus, which are part of the Laurel Highlands. In the vicinity mixed hardwoods grow and also such southern species as the distinctive umbrella magnolia (*Magnolia tripetala*) with its ruby, cone-shaped fruit maturing in October.

In Appalachian woods, the first frost once triggered the collection of ginseng (*Panax quinquefolius*) roots, valued for their medicinal powers across the world. Too few gatherers honored the length of time it takes for a plant to grow mature roots by planting the red berries which germinate in 18 months. Pennsylvanians now need a permit to collect this species which was once common in forested uplands.

By autumn's end, Pennsylvania's rich deciduous forests have gained another year's growth and have lost a season's foliage. Nature's palette in October is now replaced by dappled browns. By December the forest seems temporarily drained of vigor. Some tree trunks have been permanently marked by "buck rub" if male deer scraped the bark to remove the velvet from their mature antlers. Most seeds have found a home or at least a resting spot for continuous cold. To keep warm, I savor images of the Alleghenies, the Laurel Highlands and the Blue Mountain while their fall foliage was at its peak.

ABOVE This upland forest of mixed hardwoods and white pines produces fall foliage visible from Interstate 80 near State College, Centre County. RIGHT This fast-flowing stream and moss-covered rocks are part of the beauty of Quehanna Wild Area, State Forest Land, Cameron County in northcentral Pennsylvania.

LEFT AND ABOVE The West Branch of the
Susquehanna River flows through second-growth
forests that were heavily logged in the mid-1800s when
the state was first in lumber production. The woods
along Route 120 which threads through Clinton,
Cameron and Elk Counties confirm that Penn's Woods
is still an apt description for the state. Pennsylvania has
8.9 million acres of timberland within its 17 million
acres of forestland.

PREVIOUS PAGES Hay-scented ferns (*Dennstaedtia punctilobula*), golden from lack of chlorophyl, cover the ground under a stand of hardwoods at Cameron County's Quehanna, one of the state's 44 Wild Areas. ABOVE Among wetland plants in The Black Moshannon Bog Natural Area in Centre County are leatherleaf (*Chamaedaphne calyculata*) and waterlilies (*Nymphaea* spp.) RIGHT Within nature's biodiversity, death sustains life and often creates artistry during the process, Black Moshannon State Park.

• • • • • • • • • • • • • •

LEFT A doe (*Odocoieleus virginianus*) and two young white-tailed deer stand watchfully at forest edge, Black Moshannon State Park, Centre County. Among the 15,000 species of wildlife in Pennsylvania, deer are both popular and populous. It is easy to sight this graceful mammal. Prior to the state's annual hunting season, the deer population tops a million. The number has steadily increased since colonial days because deer thrive in disturbed environments, especially where food crops occur. In deep forests where scarcity of food may affect nutrition, fewer fawns grow to the size of these twins. ABOVE Clarion River flows through the middle of Elk County.

ABOVE When a milkweed (*Asclepias syriaca*) seedpod opens in the fall, downy tufts give the seeds wing. These dark seeds are ready to take to the air at Maurice C. Goddard State Park, Mercer County. RIGHT In autumn's grayness, the fall's brilliant colors soften to a healing tone, Wyoming State Forest, Sullivan County. Within its 42,000 acres such hardwoods as cherry, maple, ash and beech grow.

LEFT With an elevation of 1300 feet, the Pole Steeple
Outcrop, a metamorphic rock 500-900 million years
old, is prominent in this aerial view of Pine Grove
Furnace State Park, which is located in the Michaux State
Forest, Cumberland County. Oaks are dominant among
these mixed hardwoods. ABOVE The colors of leaf litter
in the fall mimic the brillance of the overhead canopy.
Bright fungi such as this mushroom sprout in moist
woodlands here in Bald Eagle State Forest, which
comprises almost 200,000 acres within the midstate's
sandstone ridge and valley system.

PREVIOUS PAGES This aerial view of Pine Creek
Gorge, which bisects Leonard Harrison and Colton Point
State Parks in Tioga County, features some of 2.1 million
acres set aside as state forests. ABOVE The first fork of
Sinnemahoning Creek ripples past aspens (*Populous* spp.)
through the Sinnemahoning State Park in Cameron and
Potter Counties. RIGHT During autumn the textures
and colors of the land and water blend at a wetland in
Promised Land State Park in Pike County. Vegetation
includes mats of peat moss (*sphagnum* spp.)

LEFT This fallen white pine (*Pinus strobus*) will deterio-
rate without disturbance at Heart's Content, a scenic area
with 300-year-old pines and hemlocks (*Tsuga canadensis*)
in the Allegheny National Forest, Forest County. ABOVE
In Allegheny, the state's largest forest, moss-covered (*H.
impoenes*) logs, browning ferns and fallen leaves signal
decay, a part of the woods' seasonal cycle, here in McKean
County.

PREVIOUS PAGES From High Knob Overlook in Sullivan County near the Loyalsock Trail the ridges and high plateaus of Wyoming State Forest Lands stretch endlessly. The burnished leaves in the foreground are chestnut oak (*Quercus prinus*). This vista features blooming mountain laurel in spring. ABOVE Hardwoods and hemlocks (*Tsuga canadensis*) in the Alleghenies show off their hues near Warren in the northwest. RIGHT A red maple (*Acer rubrum*) and black birch (*Betula lenta*) parade autumn along the Allegheny River in Warren County.

• • • • • • • • • • • •

PREVIOUS PAGES The mystery of an ever-flowing stream is compelling, here at Brooks Run, Elk State Forest, Cameron County. LEFT From Hyner View State Park looking north, the West Branch of the Susquehanna River bends among ridges which include parts of the Sproul State Forest, Clinton County. Purchased in 1898, Sproul is the state's oldest state forest. ABOVE The path of a brook and the natural materials that chart it are an intriguing sculpture, here in Elk State Forest Lands, Cameron County.

W I N T E R

After their brilliance during autumn, Pennsylvania's broadleaf forests retreat from growing by reposing in brown bareness. Their activities become more private as they ration their own nutrients. It is my own private pleasure to tramp through the wilds while nature pilots through sub-freezing temperatures while in neutral. I enjoy the stark textures of stiff plants that were flexible wands of color a few months ago. I note dozens of shades of brown from creamy buff to umber.

About one-fifth of Pennsylvania's mammals have migrated or are hibernating, but I still see such furbearers as rabbits and squirrels, both red and gray, scuttering in the woods. They are among the 51 mammals that are active, foraging for seeds and roots. Eighty species of animal life eat the bright red berries of the dogwood tree.

Even after frost I may see a few remnant blooms of the witch hazel (*Hamamelis virginiana*), the only tree in the state that produces its flowers and mature fruit at the same time. From each pod, two black seeds pop with enough force to send them soaring five or more feet. Naturalist Ned Smith noted in his diary **Gone For the Day** that some shot 19 feet in an indoor experiment. Appearing only after its leaves have fallen, the flowers of this late bloomer are a favorite of the ruffed grouse, Pennsylvania's state bird. Interdependence among wild things operates at high gear during this season.

Among the 115 bird species left after fall migration, such residents as bluejays and chickadees enjoy protection from the wind within the leafy branches of conifers. Each stately evergreen waxes its needles with sugary resin to safeguard them from freeze burn throughout the winter. Year round these trees shed their narrow leaves, building a spongy, slowly decomposing mat under their dark boughs. I tread almost reverently within this cathedral-like atmosphere.

In contrast, at this time of year I stomp decisively through deciduous forests, crunching through the light layer of crackly leaves. Underneath, within the moist humus at varied stages of decay is a soil factory. Ninety percent of the dry matter made by forest plants goes into decomposition. A sugar maple (*Acer saccharum*) leaf may break down within a year, but the litter from pines and larches may take three years to become soil. Its production from water, plant matter, rocks and minerals is the quintessence of life in the forest. It never stops, even in winter.

Despite so much activity, quiet reigns. And within its hallowed stillness, Pennsylvania's geological features become prominent. Scars carved by the ravages of wind, water, ice and pressure stand out in vivid relief. Hundreds of millions of years ago massive boulders were hoisted against a hillside or each other. Today pockets of soil on their surfaces may cradle tree seedlings. In many state parks e.g., Trough Creek and World's End, saplings that are four or more inches in diameter have established themselves on the tabletops of rocks.

When snow falls, the quiet deepens. The moist blanket cushions nature's few sounds. Plodding through a familiar woods newly touched by snow always surprises me. At first I am so enraptured by the beauty that it doesn't matter that I can't locate telltale characteristics of God's decor. In sub-freezing air, the falls that once poured eternally is now a partial sculpture, its energy imaginatively frozen.

Stones and tree trunks wear new faces. Swift-flowing streams and creeks absorb each snowflake, refusing to be blanketed. At their edges the powerful rush soaks icy crystals underneath layers of snow powder.

Joann Albert, a state naturalist, enjoyed hiking Somerset County's Mt. Davis after a major snowstorm. Besides being Pennsylvania's highest point, Davis rises higher than any other mountain due west to the Rockies. As a result, weather systems often unload atop its 3,213-foot summit. Albert described the setting, "Every shape had been stroked by snow crystals glistening in the sun. Cardinals flashed by in scarlet, leaving markings in the snow. Tiny tracks left by mice, grouse and other woodland species confirmed the presence of more winter residents than I could see. There were no signs of deer; perhaps they were still bedded down."

Environmental education specialist David E. Young feels drawn to lakes in winter because evaporation creates a hoarfrost on all the surrounding vegetation. "It's as though the body of water is breathing," he says. "An inch of artistic ice covers bare branches, deep green rhododendron and the winter weeds that are now skeletons."

Pennsylvania's earliest flower, skunk cabbage (*Symplocarpus foetidus*) often heralds spring when it is officially still winter. First, out pokes the flower, a rounded spadix covered with tiny flowers containing both pistils and stamens, all protected by a greenish hooded sheath. Next, pointed leaves wrapped to resemble candle flames often push through the snow. This thermo-genetic plant has adapted well to being a frontliner of the season. During its long growing season it garners nutrients via its tall, wide leaves, storing them in white roots that multiply into a mass that could barely fit in a bathroom sink. It uses this surplus over the winter, and sends up blooms that create their own heat of up to 70 degrees as early as February. Their warmth melts any precipitation around the protruding plant, making them easy to spot in a snowy woods.

A few other plants protect their nutrients from the cold by squatting close to the ground in the shape of a winter rosette. Evening primrose (*Oenothera biennis*), thistles and goldenrods practice this adaptive winterizing, often staying green until they shoot up a full-sized plant in the spring,

On early March walks I see other signs that although winter has growing on hold, it is a season of promise. Leaf scales protect barely formed buds close to branches. Deep under a foot of leaf litter, seeds rest in their protective coating. Conifer seeds snuggle inside their cones, waiting for longer days and potential germination. With majesty, the heaths poignantly hold their well-wrapped flower buds. Willing to honor the annual repose of Pennsylvania's forests, I slip away in anticipation of that cherished season, spring.

ABOVE Snow and fog add moisture to Loyalsock Creek which snakes through a narrow valley at World's End State Park, Sullivan County. RIGHT Ice and frozen snow rim a segment of Ganoga, the highest falls at Ricketts Glen State Park, Luzerne County.

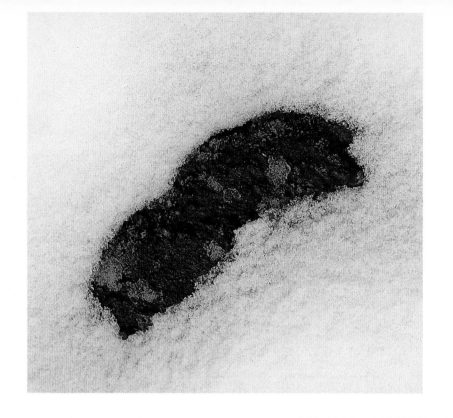

PREVIOUS PAGES Snow tops ice formations made by a stream pouring over a mountainside, World's End State Park, Sullivan County. CLOCKWISE FROM UPPER LEFT An ice-glazed rock in the snow highlights lichens that are weathering it, Pine Grove Furnace State Park, Cumberland County. • Pine (*Pinus strobus*) needles hold snow after a winter storm, Little Buffalo State Park, Perry County. • A new snowfall contrasts with hemlocks (*Tsuga canadensis*) and a dark stream at Colonel Denning State Park, Perry County.

ABOVE, LEFT TO RIGHT A heavy snowfall hides the
identifying features of a familiar woods, Michaux State
Forest in Cumberland County. • A March storm encases
red maple (*Acer rubrum*) leaf buds in snow and ice, Laurel
Ridge State Park, Westmoreland County. • Ganoga, the
94-foot falls at Ricketts Glen State Park, is framed by
winter's artistry, Luzerne County.

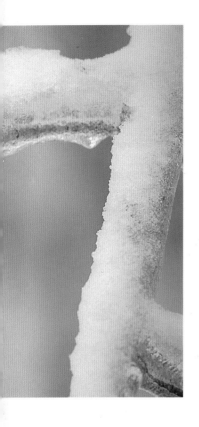

READING SOURCES

Harding, John J., ed. **Marsh, Meadow, Mountain: Natural Places of the Delaware Valley.** Philadelphia: Temple University Press, 1986. Naturalists contributed to this guide to seasonal features of habitats along the Delaware River, including Pennsylvania and New Jersey.

Hoffman, Carolyn **Fifty Hikes in Eastern Pennsylvania: Day Hikes and Backpacks from the Susquehanna to the Delaware.** Woodstock, VT: Backcountry Publications, 1989, 2nd ed. The first of a series of regional guidebooks to trails and natural phenomena.

Martin, Laura C. **Wildflower Folklore.** Charlotte, NC: The East Woods Press, 1984. This reference chronicles stories, historical uses and origins of wildflowers.

Oplinger, Carl S. and Robert Halma **Poconos: An Illustrated Natural History Guide.** New Brunswick: Rutgers University Press, 1988. This extensively illustrated guidebook details the development and current status of plant and animal life and geological features of the Pocono plateau.

Pennsylvania Atlas and Gazetteer. Freeport, ME: DeLorme Mapping, 1990. This large format softcover presents topographic maps of the entire state, showing all features e.g., bodies of water, altitude, back roads and outdoor recreation sites.

Pennsylvania Recreational Guide. Showing state park and forest lands and their facilities, this free map and pamphlets for individual state parks are available from Bureau of State Parks P.O. Box 1467, Harrisburg, PA 17105-1467. For information, call 1-800-63-PARKS.

Shosteck, Robert **Flowers and Plants: An International Lexicon with Biographical Notes.** New York: Quadrangle/The New York Times Book Co., 1974. Using common names alphabetically, this text documents characteristics, history and use, both culinary and medicinal.

Thwaites, Tom **Fifty Hikes in Central Pennsylvania.** Woodstock, VT: Backcountry Publications, 1985. Trail maps and how-to text guide readers to scenic views, falls and virgin timberlands.

Thwaites, Tom **Fifty Hikes in Western Pennsylvania: Walks and Day Hikes from the Laurel Highlands to Lake Erie.** Woodstock, Backcountry Publications, 1990.

Weidensaul, Scott **Seasonal Guide to the Natural Year.** Golden, CO: Fulcrum Publishing, 1992. An experienced naturalist presents a month by month guide to natural events in the Mid-atlantic Region.